IMAGES OF INDONESIA

HEINZ VON HOLZEN
FABIAN VON HOLZEN

Marshall Cavendish
Editions

© 2014 Marshall Cavendish International (Asia) Private Limited

Published by Marshall Cavendish Editions
An imprint of Marshall Cavendish International
1 New Industrial Road, Singapore 536196

Other Marshall Cavendish Offices:
Marshall Cavendish Corporation. 99 White Plains Road, Tarrytown NY 10591-9001, USA • Marshall Cavendish International (Thailand) Co Ltd. 253 Asoke, 12th Flr, Sukhumvit 21 Road, Klongtoey Nua, Wattana, Bangkok 10110, Thailand • Marshall Cavendish (Malaysia) Sdn Bhd, Times Subang, Lot 46, Subang Hi-Tech Industrial Park, Batu Tiga, 40000 Shah Alam, Selangor Darul Ehsan, Malaysia.

Marshall Cavendish is a trademark of Times Publishing Limited

National Library Board, Singapore Cataloguing-in-Publication Data:
Holzen, Heinz von, photographer.
Images of Indonesia / Heinz von Holzen and Fabian von Holzen.
– Singapore : Marshall Cavendish Editions, c2014.
pages cm
ISBN : 978-981-4516-08-2 (paperback)
1. Indonesia—Social life and customs -- Pictorial works. 2. Indonesia -- Pictorial works.
I. Title.   II. Holzen, Fabian von, photographer.
DS625
915.98 -- dc23
OCN880894319

All photographs by Heinz and Fabian von Holzen except pp 104–105 by Peter Kersten

Printed in Singapore by Craft Print International Ltd

IMAGES OF INDONESIA

CONTENTS

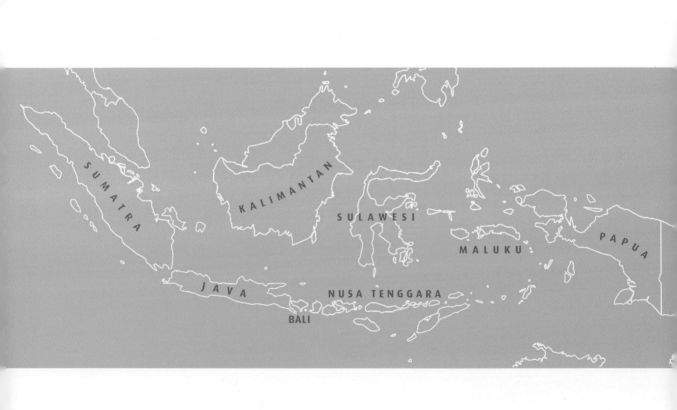

01

INTRODUCTION

With more than 18,000 islands in its territory, the country of Indonesia is the world's largest archipelago (group of islands). It abounds in natural beauty, from active volcanoes and lush tropical rainforests to a coastline of fascinating variety – all 80,000km of it. Within these islands, a rich diversity of cultures coexists, predominantly Muslim, but also many pockets of indigenous traditions. Following the end of World War II, Indonesia achieved independence from Dutch colonial rule, and is today Southeast Asia's largest economy.

THE LAND

Indonesia's geographic location at the edges of three major tectonic plates has resulted in a unique landscape – one of numerous volcanoes (including more than 130 active ones), and frequent earthquakes. The archipelago's forest, river and marine ecosystems support the world's second-highest level of biodiversity (after Brazil).

Ketapang, East Java

Kutacane, Sumatra

Mount Lompobatang, Sulawesi

Tarimbang beach, Sumba

Mount Sumbing, Central Java

Mount Slamet, Central Java

Mount Semeru, East Java

Mount Sumbing, Central Java

Kuta beach, Lombok

Lake Batur, Bali

THE PEOPLE

While Indonesia's volcanoes have wreaked frequent destruction, volcanic rocks and ash are also a source of life. They contribute to the region's highly fertile soils – a crucial factor in the flourishing of agriculture and population growth, historically and at present. The people of Indonesia, numbering over 230 million, represent some 300 native ethnic groups. And while more than 700 languages and dialects are spoken throughout the archipelago, the national language Bahasa Indonesia is taught in all schools, uniting the people by means of a common tongue.

FOOD

The food of Indonesia is a delectable blend of indigenous traditions and influences from India, China, the Middle East and Europe. Dishes like sate, rendang and soto have achieved iconic status as national foods, while lesser-known regional specialties continue to reflect the specific cultures of their birth. (*This page*) Nasi campur, a dish of rice accompanied by various sides; lontong (rice cakes), wrapped in banana leaf; (*facing page*) pisang goreng (fried banana fritters), and sate (grilled meat skewers).

SUMATRAN CUISINE

The cuisine of Sumatra often contains Middle Eastern and Indian influences, for instance in the spicy curries such as rendang sapi (braised beef with coconut and spices) and gulai kambing (mutton curry), which form the main components of Nasi Padang. Other dishes include (*facing page*) tekwan fish-ball and prawn noodle soup and Palembang beef rib soup.

JAVANESE CUISINE

Javanese cuisine is decidedly milder than Sumatran cuisine – but no less tasty. Bakso meatball soup and opor ayam (chicken in spiced coconut sauce) are two of the region's characteristic dishes.

SULAWESI CUISINE

The robust cuisine of Sulawesi includes dishes like hagape daging (spiced coconut beef), otak otak (minced fish steamed in banana leaf) and Coto Makassar (beef soup with ground peanuts).

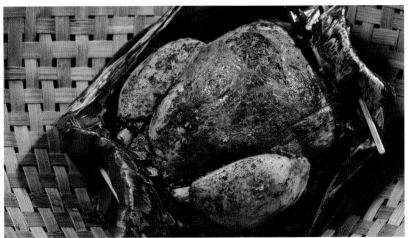

BALINESE CUISINE

The cuisine of Bali, apart from the absence of beef due to the predominantly Hindu culture, is rich in flavours and inspirations. Ayam betutu is a well-known local preparation of chicken roasted in banana leaf; other dishes include (*facing page*) chicken rice porridge as well as colourful vegetarian creations.

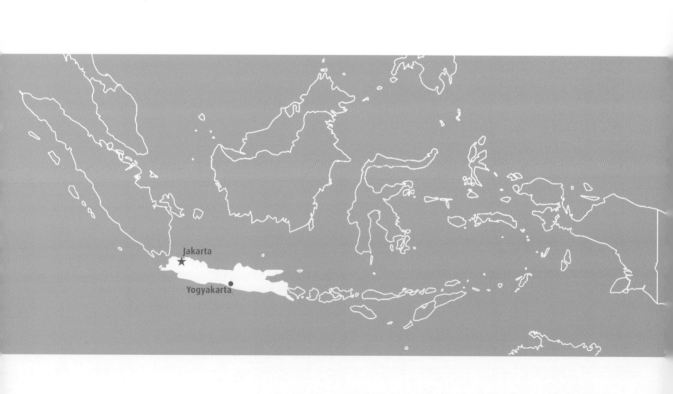

02

JAVA

The island of Java, home to 57% of Indonesia's population, is the cradle of Indonesian history. Early Hindu-Buddhist empires of the 8th to 15th century flourished here, as did the ensuing Islamic sultanates. With its fertile volcanic soil and plentiful rainfall, Java supported agriculture on a wide scale, particularly wet rice cultivation – the basis of the ancient kingdoms. Today, it is the most developed island in Indonesia, with the major cities of Jakarta, Surabaya and Bandung serving as international centres of business, trade and industry.

JAKARTA

The capital of Indonesia, Jakarta is the country's largest city, and with almost 10 million inhabitants, the most populous city in Southeast Asia. Here, the diverse cultures of the archipelago come together in a vibrant melting pot – of people, history, arts, entertainment and commerce.

NATIONAL MONUMENT

The 132m-tall Monas (Monumen Nasional) stands in the middle of Merdeka Square. Completed in 1975, this architectural icon, topped off with a symbolic golden flame, is a monument to the Indonesian people's struggle for independence from Dutch rule in the first half of the 20th century.

MERDEKA SQUARE

Jakarta's vast Merdeka ("Freedom") Square is surrounded by stately government buildings like the Merdeka Palace and National Museum. While the square's paved plaza serves to host large-scale national events, the surrounding gardens – with their ornamental fountains and lawns – are where many city-dwellers head to for breathing space, leisure and recreation.

ISTIQLAL MOSQUE

With a capacity of over 120,000 people, Istiqlal Mosque, the national mosque of Indonesia, is the largest in all of Southeast Asia. This architectural landmark is noted for two prominent features: a massive 45m-diameter dome sitting atop the prayer hall, and an elegant single minaret that echoes the towering form of the National Monument.

JAKARTA CATHEDRAL

The Jakarta Cathedral, consecrated in the year 1901, is the seat of the Roman Catholic archbishop of Jakarta. Designed in Neo-Gothic style, this striking building is capped off by a pair of spires constructed in iron that reach a height of 60m.

SUNDA KELAPA HARBOUR

Located at the mouth of Ciliwung River in north Jakarta, Sunda Kelapa harbour was instrumental to the historical growth of Jakarta as a port city – from as far back as the 13th century. Today, it serves only *pinisi* – the picturesque traditional wooden sailing ships that ply between the islands of the archipelago.

CENTRAL JAVA

Central Java is home to some of Indonesia's most awe-inspiring phenomena, both natural and manmade. Against a backdrop of lush paddy fields and volcanoes (such as the dormant Merbabu, next to the very active Merapi), the temple complexes of Borobudur and Prambanan stand out as monumental achievements of human civilisation.

YOGYAKARTA

Also known as Jogjakarta or Jogja, this historical town is a centre of Javanese arts such as traditional music, batik fabrics and wayang kulit shadow puppetry. Buildings from the time of Dutch colonialism add to the town's charm, while the shops and streetside vendors along Jalan Malioboro offer an eye-opening range of handicrafts.

KRATON PALACE

At the heart of Yogyakarta lies the Kraton (Sultan's Palace), a grand palace complex built in 1756–90 for the royal family of the Yogyakarta Sultanate. Its fine architecture, courtyards, pavilions and galleries create a tranquil atmosphere in which to explore the history of the region and enjoy traditional arts such as gamelan orchestra performances.

BOROBUDUR

The world's largest Buddhist temple, Borobudur is breathtaking in its scale, complexity, intricacy and religious/historical significance. Over 500 Buddha statues and some 2,500 stone relief panels adorn this 9th-century architectural wonder. Pilgrims ascend the complex along a path symbolising the Buddhist conception of the universe. When Java gradually converted to Islam from the 14th century, Borobudur was abandoned, and thereafter fell into obscurity – until it was "rediscovered" by Stamford Raffles in 1814.

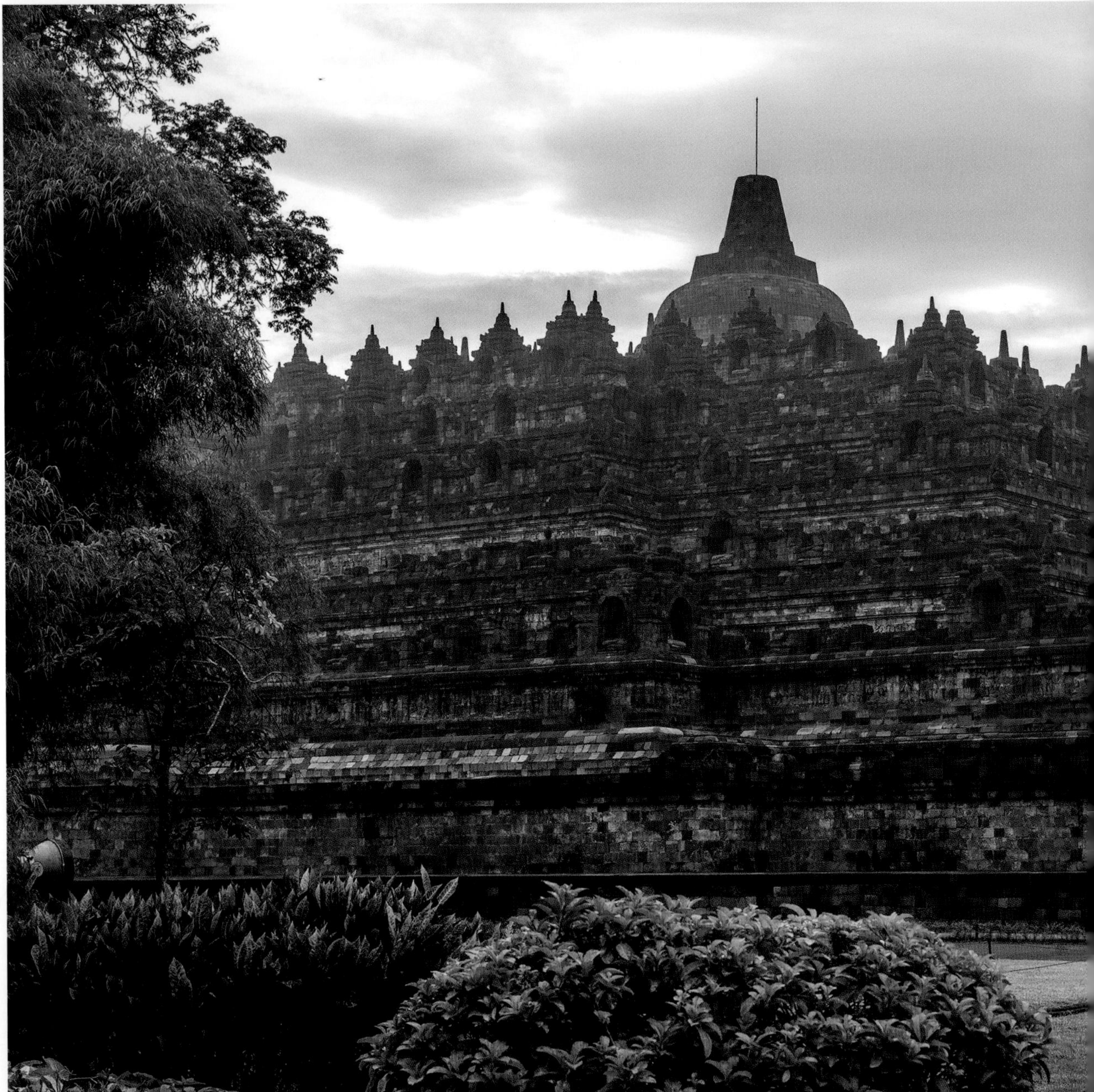

PRAMBANAN

The Hindu temple complex of Prambanan is dominated by three towering shrines, dedicated to the three great Hindu divinities – Siva, Brahma and Vishnu. Built in the 9th century (likely in response to Borobudur), this magnificent feat of stone construction collapsed in the 11th century, but reconstruction works since the 20th century have restored Prambanan's status as an important focus for Hindu rituals in Java.

DIENG PLATEAU

At 2,000 metres above sea level, the volcanic plain known as Dieng (literally "Abobe of the Gods") is a wondrous landscape of mist, sulphuric fumes and coloured lakes. Eight small Hindu shrines stand enigmatically on the plateau – the only remains of what was once a complex of hundreds of temples in the 8th century AD.

EAST JAVA

East Java, comparatively less populated than Central and West Java (albeit still the third-most populous province in Indonesia), boasts a rich diversity of landscapes: fertile fields, sandy beaches, and above all, the volcanic splendour of Bromo-Tengger-Semeru National Park.

MOUNT BROMO

One of the more easily accessible volcanoes in Java, Mount Bromo (2,329m) offers hikers a variety of terrains – from green valleys and the surrounding "Sea of Sand" to the craggy rim of the caldera. Sunrise viewed from the top is spectacular, as is the sight of neighbouring Mount Semeru's ominous plumes of white smoke.

MOUNT SEMERU

Mount Semeru, Java's highest volcano at 3,676m, has been in a state of eruption for almost 50 years now, with ash explosions occuring every 10–30 minutes. This sublime, mythical landscape draws visitors, trekkers and religious pilgrims from all over the world.

IJEN SULPHUR MINES

The volcano Ijen is the site of the largest highly-acidic crater lake in the world, where sulphur is still mined using traditional, back-breaking methods. Workers transport the chunks of solid sulphur using baskets – the loads weighing up to 90kg – from the lake up to the crater rim, a vertiginous ascent of some 300m, at gradients as steep as 60 degrees.

BALI

03 BALI

Although geographically part of the grouping known as the Lesser Sunda Islands, Bali occupies a unique place all its own, in terms of history, culture and international recognition. The population is predominantly Hindu – an anomaly in Muslim-majority Indonesia – and religious beliefs suffuse all aspects of Balinese life. Hailed as the "Island of the Gods", Bali is the country's most popular tourist destination, beloved for its beaches, mountains and rich traditions in arts such as dance, music, sculpture and woodcarving.

BALI CULTURE

The vitality of Balinese culture is captivating, from the several unique styles of gamelan music to ritual dances featuring mythological creatures like Barong the king of spirits and his eternal adversary Rangda the demon queen. In everyday life, the Balinese give thanks to the gods by placing offerings in little baskets called *canang sari* in temples, at home and on the ground.

ARCHITECTURE

Rooted in Balinese Hinduism, the architecture of the island expresses the harmony between man, nature and the gods. Black thatched roofs, red-brick walls, ornate stone gateways, reflecting pools – these are architectural features that have been co-opted for tropical flavour in resorts the world over, but they must be seen in their native setting here to be fully appreciated.

BEACH LIFE

Bali, with its warm water and good waves, is one of the world's top destinations for surfing. The island's many beaches – from vibrant Kuta to exclusive Nusa Dua – are also excellent for swimming and sailing, as well as just chilling out, enjoying a seafood meal, and watching the sun set over the water.

SALT-MAKING AT AMED

Amed, a string of coastal villages in Bali's northeast increasingly being developed for tourism, is known for its production of sea salt. Rows of drying pans can be seen on the beaches, where seawater slowly evaporates to leave behind salt crystals that are then harvested for sale.

PEOPLE

Life in Bali proceeds at a leisurely pace even away from the beaches and temples. Exploring the towns is made all the more pleasurable by the warmth and friendliness of the locals.

MOUNTAINS AND LAKES

The highest point on Bali island is Mount Agung (3,148m), an active volcano considered sacred by the Balinese, while the largest body of water is Lake Batur (18 sq m), formed in the old crater of Mount Batur.

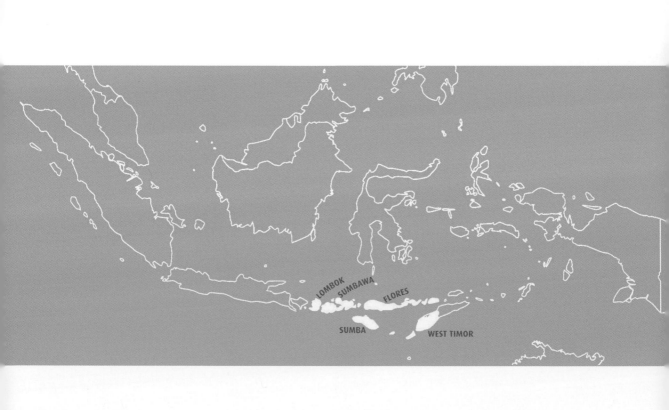

04

NUSA TENGGARA

Also known as the Lesser Sunda Islands, Nusa Tenggara encompasses the major islands of Lombok, Sumbawa, Flores, Sumba and hundreds of other smaller ones. The western half of Timor island also belongs in this grouping, while the eastern half is the independent nation of Timor-Leste (East Timor). Rich in flora and fauna, and diverse in culture and history, the islands of Nusa Tenggara are starting to get their due attention from travellers seeking an alternative to the much-trodden paths of neighbouring Bali.

LOMBOK

Lombok is often called the "Island of 1000 Mosques". Located to the immediate east of Bali, it is an island of tranquil, natural beauty, with sandy beaches, forests and waterfalls – all easily enjoyed within easy access from the resorts clustered primarily around Senggigi township. The island's fertile soil is cultivated with rice, spices, coffee and coconuts.

KUTA BEACH

Kuta Beach, on the south coast of Lombok (not to be confused with the beach of the same name in Bali), boasts crystal-clear waters and pristine white sand.

MOUNT RINJANI

The second-highest volcano in Indonesia, Mount Rinjani rises to a majestic height of 3,726m. Climbing to the crater rim is a challenging 2-day trek; from there, a breathtaking view is afforded of the surroundings, and of the crater lake whose blue water, so reminiscent of the sea, earned it the name Segara Anak ("Child of the Sea").

SUMBAWA

East of Lombok is the larger but comparatively less developed island of Sumbawa, characterised by its rugged terrain, thick vegetation, indigenous cultural practices and a slow, unhurried pace of life.

FLORES

As a result of its colonisation by Portugal, Flores is predominantly Roman Catholic. Picturesque churches dot the island, and Larantuka is especially noted for its festivities during Holy Week. The village of Bena boasts Stone Age megaliths and traditional houses characteristic of the local Ngada culture.

IKAT DYEING AND WEAVING

Handwoven ikat fabrics are one of the cultural treasures of Indonesia, the designs varying from region to region. Without the use of any modern machinery, the artisans go through a painstaking process of spinning, dyeing and weaving, to produce these intricate works of wearable art.

SUMBA

Traditional architecture on the island of Sumba reflects both spiritual and pragmatic concerns. The characteristic thatched roof, which can be as high as 30m, represents the hair and head of a human, while the four main columns represent the legs. Within the high roof, rice and corn are stored, where the smoke from the kitchen beneath helps to keep the grains dry.

PASOLA
FESTIVAL

The most spectacular ceremonial festival on Sumba is the Pasola, an annual ritual battle fought with spears featuring hundreds of horsemen. Blood spilled in battle is believed to fertilise the ground on which it falls, promising a bountiful harvest to come.

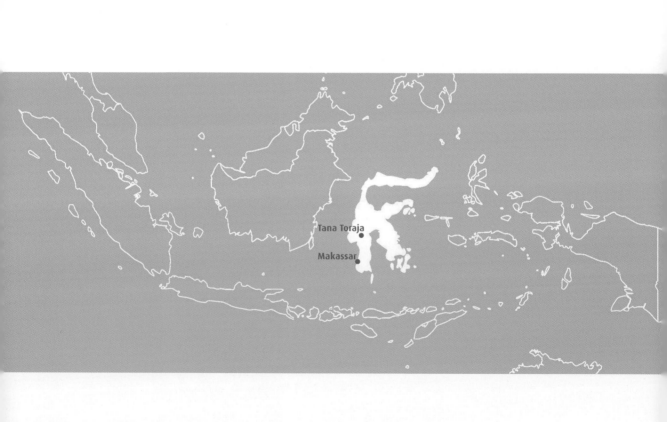

Tana Toraja

Makassar

05

SULAWESI

With its four peninsulas stretching out to form what looks like a letter "k", the island of Sulawesi is always recognisable. The people are predominantly Muslim, though the Toraja ethnic group accounts for a significant Christian population. The southwest of the island is the homeland of the Bugis, whose diaspora can be found all over Southeast Asia. In former times, Sulawesi was known as Celebes.

SULAWESI

A wealth of diverse landscapes can be found on the sprawling island of Sulawesi – mountains, coffee plantations, forest parks, beaches, and some world-class diving spots.

MAKASSAR

The largest city on Sulawesi is Makassar, which has played a significant role in the region's history as a trading port. Guarding the harbour is Fort Rotterdam, an old fortress dating back to the Dutch colonial era.

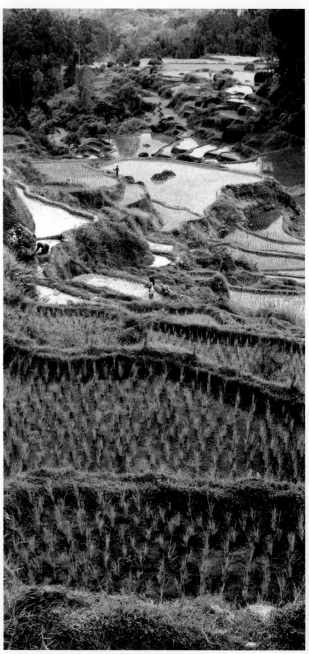

TANA TORAJA

Tana Toraja ("Land of Toraja") is the homeland of the Toraja people, indigenous to South Sulawesi, who are renowned for their traditional architecture – houses with dramatically sweeping roofs – as well as their burial sites carved into rocky cliffs, guarded by life-size wooden effigies.

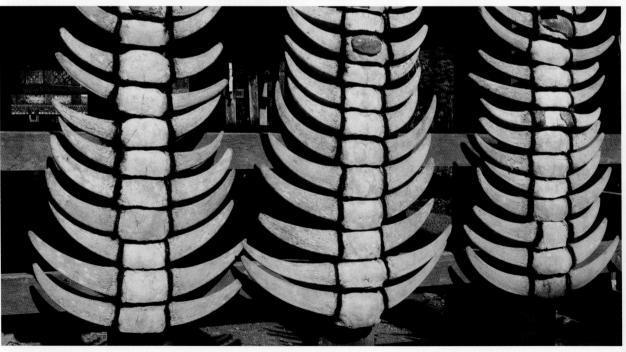

PINISI SHIPBUILDING

In South Sulawesi, a traditional shipbuilding craft survives. The pinisi is a two-masted sailing ship, the first examples of which were introduced by the Dutch in the 17th century. These elegant wooden vessels are used today mostly for transporting cargo between the islands of the Indonesian archipelago.

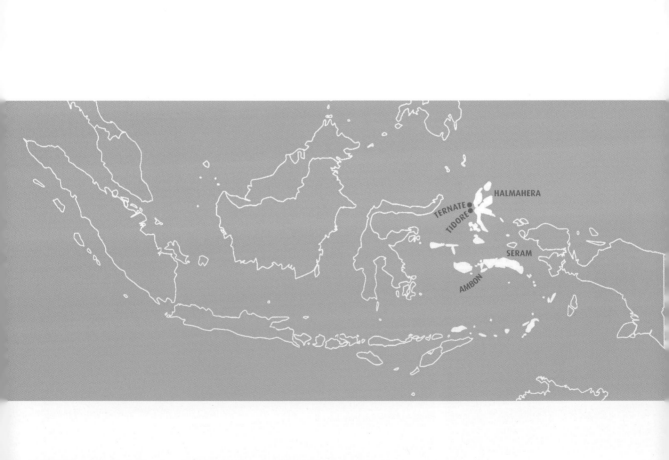

These are the famous "Spice Islands" that drew the Europeans to this part of the world from the 16th century, to participate in the lucrative trade in spices like nutmeg and cloves – which could only be found here. More than 1,000 islands make up Maluku. The largest are Halmahera and Seram, though the most developed are the small islands of Ternate and Ambon.

06 MALUKU (MOLUCCAS)

TERNATE AND TIDORE

The small, cone-shaped island of Ternate was once – together with its neighbour and historical rival Tidore – the world's single major producer of cloves. Today, one finds vestiges of its past in colonial constructions such as Fort Tolukko and Fort Oranye (built by the Dutch East Indies Company).

28 PEBRUARI 1570

SPICES

In the days before refrigeration, spices were highly sought after for their ability to preserve food, as well as for their medicinal properties. This drew traders – European, Chinese, Arab, Indian – to the only place the spices were known to grow. Although they are now grown elsewhere in the world, cloves, nutmeg and cinnamon are still cultivated in a big way in the Maluku islands.

07

SUMATRA

Of all the islands that belong entirely to Indonesia, Sumatra is the largest, covering some 480,000 sq km. Sumatra is home to around 22% of Indonesia's population – they are largely Muslim, but represent a diverse mix of ethnic groups, including the Minangkabau, Batak and Aceh peoples. Running down the length of the island is the Bukit Barisan mountain range, which features volcanoes and tropical pine forests.

WEST SUMATRA

Facing out onto the Indian Ocean, West Sumatra is a land rich in natural wonder – beaches, forests and mountains coming together in a dramatic composition. This region is the homeland of the Minangkabau people, who are noted for their architecture, arts, illustrious diaspora, and matrilineal customs (by which land and property are passed down from mothers to daughters).

PADANG

Padang is the largest city on Sumatra's west coast, and is above all associated with its cuisine. Rice is the staple, but the chief ingredient is invariably chili – used in myriad ways to impart spice and fire to a wide array of accompanying dishes.

SOUTH SUMATRA

Indonesia is the world's fourth-largest producer of coffee, most of it grown by smallholders. Sumatran coffee is well-regarded internationally for its smoothness and intensity. At the foot of Mount Dempo in South Sumatra, the region of Pagar Alam produces a fine bean.

PALEMBANG

One of the oldest cities in Indonesia, Palembang's heyday was as the capital of the ancient Srivijaya Kingdom that once held sway over much of archipelago Southeast Asia. Today its main commerce and attractions cluster around the Musi River.

FORESTS AND WILDLIFE

Once covered by lush tropical rainforest, Sumatra has lost almost 50% of its forests in the last 40 years due to economic development and illegal logging. Many of the island's animal species have also become critically endangered, including the Sumatran Tiger and Sumatran Orang Utan. This is not confined to Sumatra, but is a problem throughout Indonesia. Although measures have been taken by the government to protect the country's natural landscape, flora and fauna, degradation continues apace.

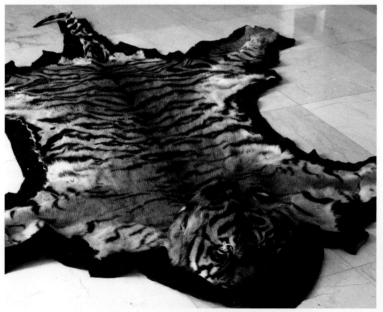

ABOUT THE AUTHORS

Heinz von Holzen is a Swiss-born entrepreneur, chef, restaurateur, hotelier, adventurer and photographer. In 1990, after having lived for several years in Singapore, Heinz moved to Bali as Executive Chef at the Grand Hyatt, and later joined the Ritz-Carlton hotel. In his quest to discover and document the richness of the cuisines of Indonesia, Heinz began to travel extensively all over the country; his growing interest in the diverse cultures of the country soon took him high up to the peaks of active volcanoes and deep into the heart of remote villages. These journeys yielded the stunning images of the vast archipelago that are presented here in this book.

Today, Heinz runs two restaurants in Bali – the award-winning Bumbu Bali Restaurant & Cooking School, and Pasar Malam, a traditional market restaurant – as well as Rumah Bali, a modern Balinese-style bed and breakfast. He is the author of numerous books, including *Step-by-Step Cooking Indonesian*, *Street Foods of Bali* and *Images of Bali*.

Fabian von Holzen picked up his father's passion for photography at the age of fourteen, and in the seven years since has channelled that passion into capturing the kaleidoscopic beauty of the land and its people on camera. After studying multimedia production in Australia, Fabian returned to Bali, where he now runs his own production company From the Woods Productions, specialising in video and photography.